Oceans

John Baines

Wayland

Our Green World

Acid Rain
Atmosphere
Deserts
Farming
Oceans
Polar Regions
Rainforests
Recycling
Wildlife

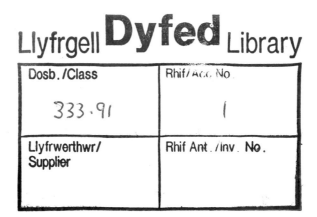
Cover: A brown pelican with a jumping shoal of fish.

Book editor: Paul Bennett
Series editor: Philippa Smith
Series designer: Malcolm Walker

First published in 1992 by
Wayland (Publishers) Ltd
61 Western Road, Hove
East Sussex BN3 1JD, England

British Library Cataloguing in Publication Data
Baines, John
Oceans. – (Our green world)
I. Title II. Series
304.2'8

ISBN 0-7502-0327-7

Typeset by Kudos Editorial and Design Services, Sussex, England
Printed in Italy by G. Canale & C.S.p.A., Turin
Bound in France by AGM

Contents

Words printed in **bold** in the main text are explained in the glossary on page 46.

An amazing world

The planet on which we live is called Earth, but almost three-quarters of it is covered by water. For every 100 litres of water there are on the Earth, 90 of them are in the seas and oceans.

The ocean bed has mountains, valleys and flat plains, and many of them are much larger than those found on the land.

▲ *From space the oceans look blue and the clouds look white.*

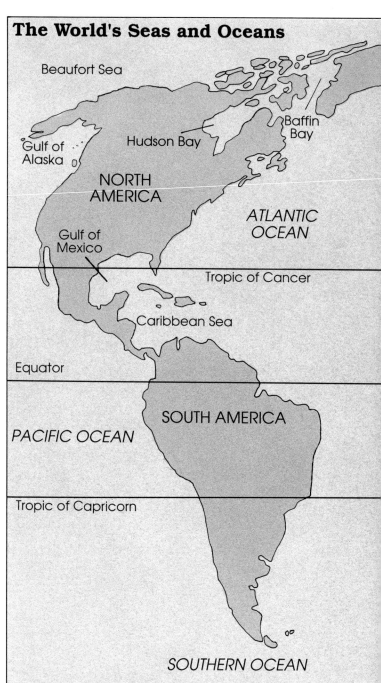

The World's Seas and Oceans

Beaufort Sea

Gulf of Alaska

Hudson Bay

Baffin Bay

NORTH AMERICA

ATLANTIC OCEAN

Gulf of Mexico

Tropic of Cancer

Caribbean Sea

Equator

PACIFIC OCEAN

SOUTH AMERICA

Tropic of Capricorn

SOUTHERN OCEAN

The oceans are a fascinating world and we still have a lot to learn about them. In this book you will find out more about the oceans, how we use them, and why we should take more care of them.

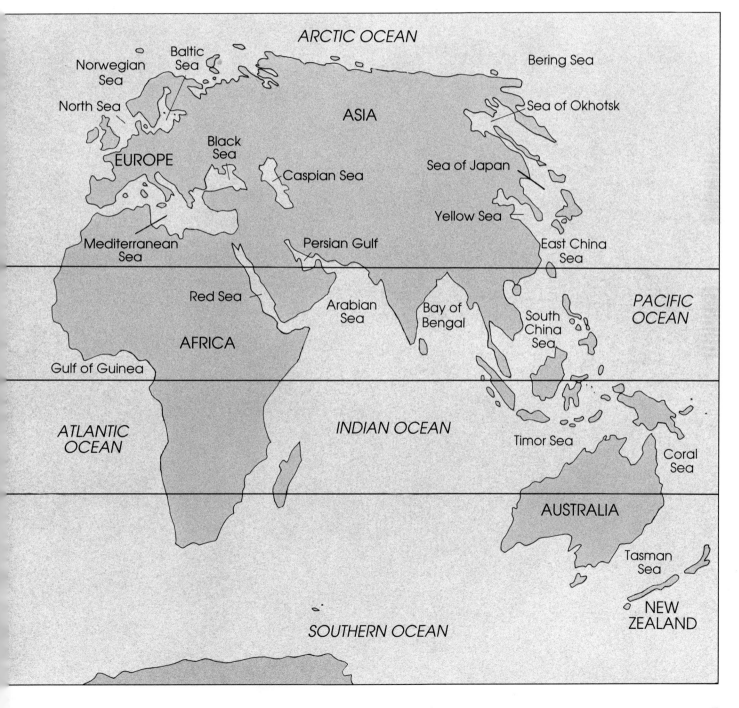

▼ *The islands of Hawaii are actually the tops of mountains rising 10,000 m above the **sea-bed**.*

The sea is full of wonderful creatures such as this clown fish. ▶

Facts and figures

Ocean/Sea	Area (sq km)	Average depth (m)	Deepest part (m)
Pacific Ocean	165,721,150	4,200	10,860
Atlantic Ocean	81,660,100	3,920	8,385
Indian Ocean	73,444,600	3,962	7,450
Arctic Ocean	14,351,200	1,280	5,334
Mediterranean Sea	2,965,550	1,371	4,593
South China Sea	2,318,000	1,646	5,016
Caribbean Sea	1,942,500	2,560	7,239
Gulf of Mexico	1,813,000	1,432	3,732
East China Sea	1,243,200	185	2,719
Hudson Bay	1,222,500	134	258
North Sea	572,390	54	659
Red Sea	461,000	454	2,834
Black Sea	436,415	1,310	2,243
Baltic Sea	409,220	67	426

The valuable oceans

Life began in the oceans many millions of years ago. Today the oceans are home to countless plants and animals. The smallest of these are called plankton. They are too tiny to see, but they are food for crabs, starfish, shrimps and even huge whales.

This colourful sea slug lives only in warm seas. ▶

▲ *The graceful manta ray is a type of shark.*

◄ *This small file fish lives among coral reefs.*

Fish are found in every ocean. They breathe the oxygen in the water. There are more types of fish than any other animal. Seabirds flying above the oceans dive into the water to catch fish. Fish are also an important source of food for people.

▲ *Sea lions catch fish in the sea, but breed on the land.*

Mammals and **reptiles** need air to breathe, but some are able to live in the sea. Whales and dolphins spend all their lives in the sea. They come to the surface every now and then to take a breath of air. Turtles swim huge distances. When it is time to lay their eggs, they return to the same beaches where they hatched.

Marine iguanas are reptiles which spend time in the sea and on land. They dive into the sea to feed on seaweed. ▶

▼ Penguins on the coast in New Zealand. Penguins are excellent swimmers, but cannot fly.

As the wind blows over the sea, it makes waves. When the waves reach the land they break against it and make cliffs and beaches. The movement of the waves can be used to make electricity.

▼ *Waves break at the shore when the sea becomes shallow.*

▲ *At La Rance in France the tides are used to make electricity.*

The tides

The tides are caused by the sun and the moon. They pull the water in the oceans towards them, making the water bulge on either side of the Earth. The bulge is biggest when the sun and moon pull in the same direction.

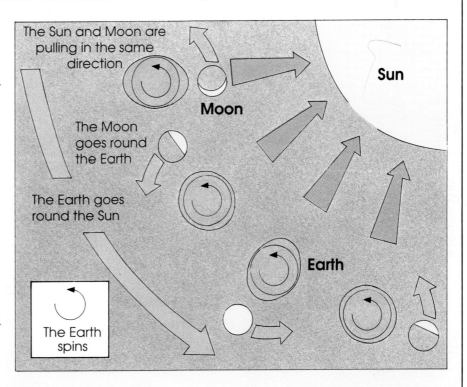

The Sun and Moon are pulling in the same direction

Moon

Sun

The Moon goes round the Earth

The Earth goes round the Sun

The Earth spins

Earth

The water in the oceans does not stay in the same place. The water at the surface is blown by the wind and moves round in great circles between the land masses. Ocean currents may be warm or cold.

The **climate** of Europe is mild and wet because the warm water of the Gulf Stream flows towards Europe.

▼ *A map to show the warm and cold currents of the world's oceans.*

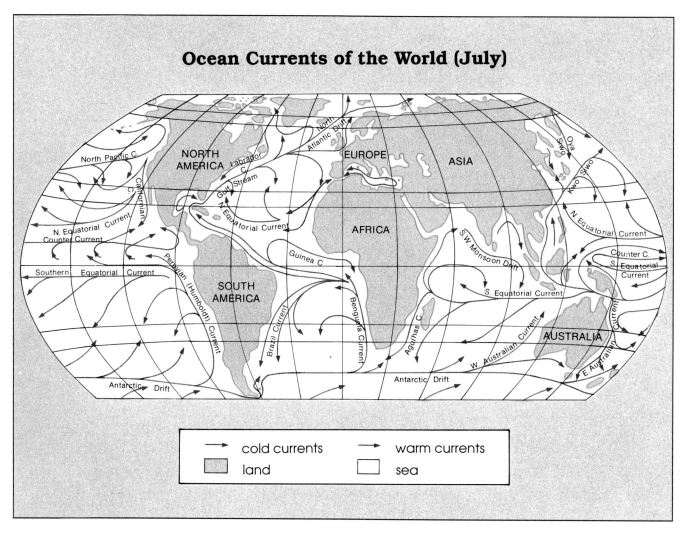

Ocean Currents of the World (July)

▲ *A drilling rig collects oil from below the sea-bed.*

The oceans are huge hollows in the land that have filled with water. The rocks at or below the sea-bed contain **resources** that we can use, just like the rocks on the land. Oil is pumped from below the sea-bed, and sand and gravel are dug up from the sea-bed.

The oceans and pollution

Plants and animals living in the oceans need clean water to stay healthy.

How do the oceans become dirty? The answer is that people dump **waste** in them. The sea is dirtiest near land, especially those areas where a lot of people live. What kind of dirt goes into the sea?

▼ *Sewage is going straight into the sea at this site near Wellington in New Zealand.*

▲ *Waste from a **fertilizer** factory in West Africa is pumped into the sea.*

Sewage is the waste that comes from our lavatories, baths, showers and sinks. It is carried away in underground pipes. Some of the pipes lead straight to the sea shore and the sewage runs into the sea.

Factories make the goods we want to buy. But factories always produce some waste. Some of this waste is dumped into the sea. There may be poisonous **chemicals** in the waste that will harm living things.

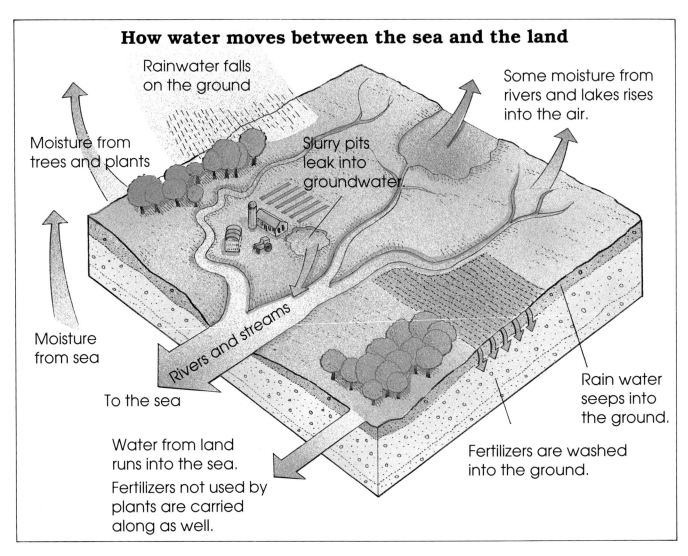

How water moves between the sea and the land

Rainwater falls on the ground

Some moisture from rivers and lakes rises into the air.

Moisture from trees and plants

Slurry pits leak into groundwater.

Moisture from sea

Rivers and streams

To the sea

Water from land runs into the sea.
Fertilizers not used by plants are carried along as well.

Rain water seeps into the ground.

Fertilizers are washed into the ground.

▲ *Farming can cause pollution in rivers and the sea.*

Farms can also **pollute** the sea. Fertilizers put on to the land, chemical sprays used on crops, and waste from animals can find their way into rivers which flow into the sea.

About six million tonnes of oil pollute the sea each year. Most comes from oil refineries and ships. It is also washed off the roads by rain, and runs down into pipes that may lead to the sea. Pollution also comes from waste dumped at sea, and from special ships which burn waste at sea.

◀ *Rubbish dumped on a beach in the Canary Islands. Turtles try to lay their eggs on this beach.*

Radioactive waste

Radioactive materials help us in all kinds of ways. They are used to make x-rays in hospitals, and to produce electricity in power stations. The radiation from them can sometimes cause diseases such as cancer.

Waste water from a nuclear factory at Sellafield, England, goes into the Irish Sea. The waste water contains tiny amounts of radioactive materials. Some people say the waste causes cancers among people living by the Irish Sea.

▲ *Greenpeace has helped to stop radioactive materials from being dumped in the sea.*

◀ *Black, sticky oil washed up on a beach is unpleasant for people, and can harm wildlife.*

The seaside and the beach are places that people enjoy visiting. Many seaside towns depend on the money that these visitors spend. The holiday-makers will stay away if the water is polluted, and sewage, oil, broken glass and other rubbish is washed up on the beach.

Some places forbid dogs to go on the beach because they may leave their droppings there.

Polluted sea water is dangerous. Sewage in the sea is the main problem because it can make people ill. Most people think the sea water at popular European beaches is safe. But some beaches have to be closed when the pollution gets too bad.

▼ *This person is collecting sea-water. It will be tested to see if it is polluted.*

The sea is an important source of food. Many people make a living from supplying sea food. Shellfish are easily affected by pollution. In some areas they are unsafe to eat.

▼ *Seafood is very good for you — as long as it is not poisoned by pollution!*

▲ *Pollution has made the shellfish found at this beach unsafe to eat.*

▲ *How sad it would be if pollution killed the wonderful wildlife found in the sea.*

It is not only people and shellfish that suffer from pollution. Some fish have become diseased, and there are fewer whales and dolphins because of polluted seas.

When oil spills into the sea, it floats on the surface. It sticks to the wings of birds and they cannot fly. Whales and seals can get covered in oil when they come to the surface to breathe.

Counting the cost
● 20 billion tonnes of waste end up in the sea every year.
● In 1988, eight in every ten seals in the North Sea died from an illness. Chemicals called PCBs may have made them less able to fight sickness.

◀ *These workers are cleaning off the oil which has stuck to the feathers of penguins.*

Chemicals in the sea

Many chemicals that are thrown away end up in the sea. Some others get there because of accidents at sea.

Many of the chemicals are poisonous. They are taken in by plants, plankton and tiny shrimp-like animals called krill. Larger animals eat these plants and animals and the poison they contain. Some of these larger animals are the fish that are caught to feed us.

We may throw our waste away in the sea, but we get it back again!

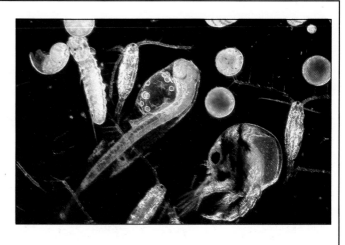

▲ *Tiny plants and animals in the sea are called plankton. Here they are seen through a microscope, which makes them look much bigger.*

Oil slick in Alaska

In March 1989 an oil tanker, called *Exxon Valdez*, set sail from an Alaskan port. It carried millions of litres of oil from Alaskan oilfields.

▲ *Oily beaches being cleaned.*

The tanker hit a reef and huge amounts of oil were spilt into the sea. It was the worst oil accident the USA has ever known. It killed thousands of fish and other animals, and polluted over 1,000 km of Alaska's coastline.

The oil company employed many people to try and clean up the beaches. Others helped to rescue wildlife. But it will take many years for the area to recover. Meanwhile, local fishermen can no longer make a living from the sea.

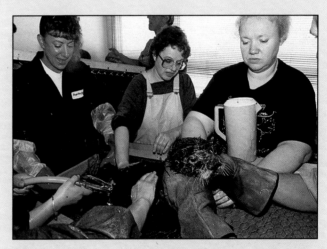

▲ *Many sea otters died, but some were saved.*

People worry that there will be other oil spill disasters. They would like to stop the drilling for oil in Alaska. They want to make Alaska a safe place for wildlife. But most of Alaska's wealth comes from the oil industry. It provides a quarter of all the oil used in the USA.

Cleaning up the oil

The worst oil pollution at sea is caused by accidents. The oil companies have several ways of dealing with oil spills. At the same time they try to reduce the damage caused to the **environment**.

▲ **Detergents** used to break up oil spills can damage wildlife.

The red booms floating on the water stop the oil spill from spreading. ▶

A small spill a long way from the shore is usually best left to break up naturally. Nearer the shore it can be:

● sprayed with detergents to make it break up quickly,
● made to sink to the bottom by spreading powdered chalk on it,
● soaked up by spongy material such as straw, or
● surrounded with barriers or booms and sucked up by another tanker.

Once the oil reaches the shore, it has to be dug up or dissolved with chemicals.

Mining and the oceans

Every day thousands of tonnes of resources are taken from under the ground and used. Coal and oil provide energy, and **ores**, such as bauxite, are made into metals.

So many of these resources have been used up that people are now looking under the sea to find more of them. Some can be found on the sea-bed, others in the rock below it.

▼ *Oil is turned into petrol and other products at refineries like this one in New Jersey, USA.*

▲ *Material from the sea-bed is being used to make dry land in Bahrain, in the Persian Gulf.*

▲ *An oil rig in the South China Sea.*

More and more oil is being taken from the rocks under
the sea. Huge drilling rigs are anchored in the sea. Great
care has to be taken so that the environment is not
damaged.

Antarctica

The Southern Ocean stretches around the continent of Antarctica. The land and the sea there contain valuable resources. However, the area is protected by the Antarctic Treaty, an agreement signed by many countries in 1959. These countries have agreed there will be no mining.

The oceans contain millions of tiny creatures we call krill. They could be caught and used for food, but what would the whales and other animals that feed on them eat instead?

◀ *The Southern Ocean is full of tiny shrimp-like creatures called krill.*

Fishing in the North Sea

Herrings used to be caught all along the east coast of Britain. The fishermen caught four million tonnes a year. However, not enough fish were left to breed. The numbers grew smaller and fishing had to be stopped to save the fish.

Scientists are trying to find out how many fish can be caught by fishermen without **overfishing**.

Fishing has gone on for thousands of years, but the oceans still contain a lot of fish. We will be able to fish for thousands more years if we do not take too many fish from the sea now.

Countries make rules to protect the fish in the waters close to their shores. However, far away from the land, large fishing fleets are emptying the oceans of fish.

Fishing is often the most important job in small coastal villages.

The victims of fishing

Fishing nets catch more than fish. Every year, about 3,000 porpoises are drowned in the North Sea. They get caught in the nets and cannot get to the surface to breathe.

Fishermen sometimes kill seals because they think that the seals eat the fish they want to catch.

▲ *This turtle is being freed from a fishing net.*

Scenes like this were common before whaling was banned. ▶

In 1988 three whales became trapped under the ice off the coast of Alaska. The television and newspapers reported their progress as people tried to rescue them. Eventually, two of them reached safety.

But over the last hundred years, humans hunted so many whales that some types are close to **extinction**. 'Save the Whale' was one of the first and most successful **environmental campaigns**. Today, only a few countries hunt whales. Eventually, the campaigners hope to stop whaling completely. They are against whaling because they believe it is wrong to harm such magnificent and intelligent creatures.

This whale was caught with a harpoon, which exploded inside it. ▶

Who owns a whale or a fish?

Countries only control what happens in the waters off their shores. No-one owns the rest of the oceans or what is in them. When fish are caught, should they belong to the fishermen, or should they belong to everyone? Should someone be able to say how many should be caught, or should people be left to do what they want?

◀ *Every year, people on the Faroe Islands, in the North Atlantic, kill thousands of pilot whales.*

Safe areas for nature

On the land there are areas where wildlife is protected, such as nature reserves and national parks. There are very few nature reserves in the sea. The largest sea reserve is Australia's Great Barrier Reef.

▼ *The Camargue is a huge area of water and land in the south of France. It has been made into a nature reserve.*

The area where a river meets the sea is called a river estuary. Estuaries are usually full of wildlife. If the river is polluted, then there is less wildlife.

Near the shore there are often flat, muddy areas called salt marshes. The tide comes in and goes out over these. Salt marshes are full of wildlife. They can make good farmland, but if the land is farmed the wildlife is lost.

Flat, muddy areas next to the sea are called salt marshes. ▶

◀ *Estuaries attract many kinds of birds.*

◀ *The mudskipper is a fish that can live in and out of the sea. It is found only in mangrove swamps.*

Mangrove swamps are the flat, marshy areas at the coast in hot countries. There is a tangle of roots which holds the trees up above the water. The swamps are full of wildlife. But people have cut down the trees for their wood, and many mangrove swamps have been destroyed.

▲ *These tourists are walking around the coastal swamps called the Everglades, in Florida, USA.*

The Great Barrier Reef

Coral reefs are made of the skeletons of millions of tiny sea creatures called polyps. They are found in warm, shallow seas and provide a home for many sea creatures.

The Great Barrier Reef is the most famous coral reef in the world. It runs for 2,000 km off the east coast of Australia. Some people wanted to look for oil there, and others wanted to dig it up to make cement. However, the reef has been made a World Heritage Site. This protects it from people — but not from the 'crown of thorns' starfish which is eating up the coral.

▲ *Can you spot which end of this butterfly fish is the front?*

◄ *A sea snake swims over Australia's Great Barrier Reef.*

The three main threats to the oceans are pollution, changes caused by such things as the building of oil rigs and **marinas**, and overfishing.

On this special ship, scientists find out more about the oceans. ▶

◀ *A researcher studying wildlife on an island on the Great Barrier Reef.*

Mussel watch

Mussels are shellfish. They can help scientists find out how polluted the water is. The mussels take in some of the pollution as they feed. The scientists collect them from time to time to see how much pollution they contain. That way they can tell if the water is getting cleaner or dirtier.

To tackle the problems, people need information about the oceans. Many countries are finding out about the seas around their shores, and international organizations are finding out about the large oceans.

Laws have been made to protect the oceans. For example, dangerous waste cannot be dumped into the sea, and oil tankers are not allowed to clean their tanks at sea.

It is very difficult to get countries to agree on how to stop overfishing. One suggestion is that the holes in fishing nets should be large enough for young fish to swim through. This will give them a chance to grow bigger and breed.

Bathers on Australia's Bondi beach. Will the world's oceans be clean enough for people to enjoy in the future?

Until recently, people were free to use the oceans in any way they wanted. Before this century, only a narrow strip of sea that stretched 4.8 km from a country's shore could be controlled by that country's government.

Today, countries are able to control what happens over a much wider strip. However, over half of the oceans are not controlled by anyone, and people are able to take as much as they want from these.

'We can no longer use the world's ocean as a dustbin.' That was said by the crew of the Greenpeace ship *Rainbow Warrior*. The ship sailed the oceans drawing attention to problems, such as pollution. Many people did not want Greenpeace to do this. Agents of the French government eventually blew up and sank the ship, killing one of the crew.

This drew people's attention to the dangers facing the oceans. All countries will have to work together to protect the oceans.

How can you help?

- Learn about the oceans.
- Join an environmental organization.
- Tell your friends why the oceans are so important.

◀ *The wreck of the Greenpeace ship* Rainbow Warrior.

Glossary

Chemicals Substances that can combine or react with each other. Many are poisonous.

Climate The weather conditions of a place or country.

Detergents Chemicals that are used for cleaning things.

Environment The surroundings in which plants and animals live.

Environmental campaigns Actions to try to save the environment of animals and plants.

Extinction When there are no animals of a particular type left.

Fertilizers Substances, such as manure or chemicals, that help the growth of plants.

Greenpeace One of the organizations which works to protect the environment.

Mammals Warm-blooded animals. The females feed their young on their own milk.

Marinas Specially-built harbours where people keep their yachts.

Ores Rocks from which metals can be made.

Overfishing This happens when more fish are taken from the sea than are replaced naturally.

Pollute To make dirty.

Radioactive materials Materials that give off invisible rays which are harmful to living things.

Reptiles Cold-blooded animals that lay eggs and have a scaly skin.

Resources Things that people use to make their lives better, such as oil and metals.

Sea-bed The bottom of the sea.

Waste Something that is not wanted any more and thrown away.

Finding out more

Books to read

The Dying Sea by Michael Bright (Franklin Watts, 1988)
Life in the Oceans by Lucy Baker (Two-Can, 1990)
Oceans and Seas by Terry Jennings (OUP, 1989)
Polluting the Sea by Tony Hare (Franklin Watts, 1990)
The Sea a series of six books from Wayland.
Whales and Dolphins & **Seals and Sea Lions**
 by Vassili Papastavrou (Wayland, 1990 and 1991)
24 hours on a Seashore by Barrie Watts (Franklin Watts, 1990)

Useful addresses

Australian Conservation
 Foundation
6726 Glenferrie Road
Hawthorn
Victoria 3122
Australia

Coastwatch UK
Farnborough College of
 Technology
Boundary Road
Farnborough
Hampshire GU14 6SB

Environmental and
 Conservation Organizations
 of New Zealand
PO Box 11057
Wellington
New Zealand

Friends of the Earth (UK)
26-28 Underwood Street
London N1 7JQ

Greenpeace (Australia)
310 Angas Street
Adelaide 5000

Greenpeace (Canada)
427 Bloor Street West
Toronto, Ontario

Greenpeace (UK)
Canonbury Villas
London N1 2PN

Marine Conservation Society
4 Gloucester Road
Ross-on-Wye
Herefordshire HR9 5BU

Index

Picture acknowledgements
Bruce Coleman Ltd 8 above, 10 (Lanting), 11 above (Ziesler), 21 (Hughes), 22 above (Hans Reinhard), 25 (Bingham), 26 above (Cubitt), 29 (Townsend), 33 (Everson), 34 (Alexander), 35 above (Boulton), 39 above (Dore), 40 above (Compost), 41 below (Roessler); Greenpeace 20 (Gleizes); Hutchison Library 44 (Hall); Natural Science Photos 42 (Ken Cole); Oxford Scientific Films *cover* (P & W Ward), 6 (Sandved), 8 below (Hauser), 9 (Zell), 11 below, 16 and 45 (Westerskov), 13, 23 and 38 (Toms), 15 (Lockwood), 19 (Cayless), 24 above (Birkhead), 26 below (Parks), 28 (Perrins), 30, 35 below (Merlen), 36 and 37 above (Martin), 39 below (Walsh), 41 above (Leszczynski), 42 above; Rex Features 27 above (Orth), and below (Today); Paul Seheult 22 (below); ZEFA 4, 7 (W Townnsend Jnr), 12 (James), 17 (Boutin), 24 below, 31 Moloney, 32 (Bingel), 37 below (Ferchland), 40 below. The illustrations are by Marilyn Clay on pages 4-5, 13 and 14, and by Stephen Wheele on page 18.